MW00966242

MOTHEI
anu
FATHER'S DAY

PROGRAM BUILDER No. 8

Recitations—Exercises—Plays
Readings—Songs

Compiled by **Diane K. Cunningham**

For the most practical use of this material, we suggest you obtain at least three copies. Photocopying of copyrighted material is not allowed.

Scripture marked NIV is from *The Holy Bible, New International Version,* copyright © 1973, 1978, 1984 by the International Bible Society. Used by permission.

Recitations & Readings

Teddy's Wish

(Small boy carrying a teddy bear)

I like my teddy bear a lot
So I brought him to say
To every mother everywhere,
"A Happy Mother's Day!"

—*Phyllis C. Michael*

Isn't She Grand?

Millions of mothers,
All fine and all dear;
Thousands of mothers,
A few of them here.

Hundreds of mothers
Across the land;
(Pointing to own mother)
See that one mother;
My! Isn't she grand?

—*Helen Kitchell Evans*

I Love Them

I help Mother,
Daddy too,
With many things
They have to do.

To show my love
For them, you see,
Because I know
They both love me.

—*Merle Glasgow*

Best Mother

I think my mother's pretty.
She has a smiling face.
I couldn't find a nicer mom
If I looked every place.

—*Velda Blumhagen*

Thanks, God

My mother is the very best
A child has ever had.
When God arranged that I'd have
mine
He surely made me glad.

—*Ruth McFadden Svec*

Both of Us Do

(For primary girl with "mama" doll)

Now just you sit there nice and still!
(Speaks to doll placed on chair)
Don't move an arm or leg until
I've said my piece and made my bow.
(Bows.)
OK. I'll go and get you now,
And you can speak your piece for us.
Now do it nice without a fuss;
Just make a bow and say, "Ah, . . . ah
(Pause to think.)
Whom do you love? *(Doll: "Ma-ma!")*

—*Phyllis C. Michael*

2

Making It Special

(For a child who carries a red rose)

I brought for my mommy
This big red rose.
How much I love her
I'm sure she knows.

But I wanted to make
It real special today
So I came up here
To tell her this way.

—*Merle Glasgow*

Three Roses

(For a child who carries three roses)

Three roses for my mommy;
They say to her today
That I love her very much
In a very special way.

—*Merle Glasgow*

My Mother

My mother tucks me in at night,
  She hears my problems and my
    prayers,
She says, "I love you," turns out the
    light
Then quietly goes downstairs.

Her loving hands are ever ready
  To work for me each day;
Her love for me is strong and steady,
  She leads me in the Christian way.

I'm here today to give God praise,
  And present this small bouquet;
May God bless my mother always,
  Today and every day.

—*Helen Kitchell Evans*

One of the Greatest

Many great gifts
  Have come from heaven above.
One of the greatest of these
  Is a mother's love.

—*Beverly Ann Hoffeditz*

Something to Be Thankful For

When I climb into bed at night
And Mother tucks the covers tight
I'm just as thankful as can be
That God sent her to live with me.

—*Phyllis C. Michael*

Good Advice

(An exercise for six boys)

BOY 1: I wonder how a little lad
       Can make his mother's heart
       real glad.

BOY 2: I wonder just what I can do
       To prove my love is all true
       blue.

BOY 3: She works real hard for me
       each day.
       Now how can I this care re-
       pay?

BOY 4: Well, as for me, it is my plan
       To grow to be a real good man.

BOY 5: I would, too, if I knew how.
       I'd start in doing that right
       now.

BOY 6 *(addressing* BOY 5):
       If you mean all the things you
       say,
       I'll tell you a simple way.
       Always be real sure to do
       Just what your mother wants
       you to.

—*Carolyn R. Freeman*

Mothers Love Us

(Tune: "Jesus Love Me")

Mothers love us, this is true,
You just watch them, you'll know too.
See them wipe away our tears,
Hold our hands to calm our fears.

Yes, mothers love us,
Yes, mothers love us,
Yes, mothers love us,
We know that this is true.

Mothers love us without praise,
They don't wait for special days.
They just love us every hour,
Teach us faith in God's great power.

—Helen Kitchell Evans

Thank You, Jesus

(For a child who speaks as if praying)

Dear Lord Jesus up in heaven,
On this happy day of days
I can see Your lovingkindness
In so many different ways.

I am grateful for all blessings
That have brought me joy and
cheer,
But especially I thank You
For my precious mother dear.

—Carolyn R. Freeman

My Choice

Mother, you're the dearest one
Of all the folks I know;
You do the nicest things for me,
Kind deeds that grow and grow.

I can't begin to name them all;
I never would get through;
And so I'll just say that for my own
mother
I'm glad that I chose you.

—Phyllis C. Michael

I Chose Love

*(For a child who carries a placard with
the word "Love" printed on it. Child
holds placard at side while speaking.)*

A gift for my mother,
Very special must be,
Because she's the dearest
Of mothers to me.

With the gift I have chosen
So happy she'll be.
It will last all the year
(Show placard to audience.)
'Cause it's "Love," you see.

—Merle Glasgow

Someone

Someone meets me every day
When I come in from school or play;
Someone smiles and hugs me tight;
Someone prays with me at night;
Someone has a great big jar
Where all the nicest cookies are;
Someone hears me when I call;
Someone helps me when I fall;
Someone always has a kiss—
Now who could be as nice as this?

Who could it be? I'm sure you know,
It is my mother who loves me so.

—Elizabeth Jones

Love like This

A mother's love
Can never be measured.
Love like this
Is doubly treasured.

—Rega Kramer McCarty

4

The Things We Owe
Our Mothers

(An exercise for four children)

1ST CHILD:
I owe my happiness to Mother.
  Without her always there
I'd be very lonely
  And have no loving care.

2ND CHILD:
I owe my many comforts
  To Mother dear, that's sure;
Whatever troubles I may have
  Her love will always cure.

3RD CHILD:
I owe my health to Mother;
  She watches over me.
I never have the slightest need
  That she isn't quick to see.

4TH CHILD:
I owe my faith to Mother;
  She taught me how to pray.
She talks to me of Jesus
  And leads me in His way.

UNISON:
We owe more things to Mother
  Than we really can recall
And we want to offer loving thanks
  For mothers, one and all.

—*Rega Kramer McCarty*

I Do Mean It!

I've said it and said it and said it,
  But I think I will say it some more;
I love you, I love you, dear Mother,
  Yes, you are the one I adore!
I've said it because I do mean it—
  No one is as precious as you.
I love you, I love you, dear Mother,
  I love you, I love you, I do!

—*Dorothy Conant Stroud*

Mother's Day

A day in May is set apart
  That we may tribute pay
To one so dear to every heart
  And we call it "Mother's Day!"

We honor heroes every day
  In one way or another,
But this one day is set apart
  Especially for Mother!

—*Nona Keen Duffy*

Faith of the Mothers

When mothers pray as Hannah
    prayed
  Then boys are born as Samuel,
A lad who listens to God's voice,
  God's message as a man will tell,
A prophet sent to warn the lost,
  A preacher making God's will done.
He lived by faith and prayer because
  He was a praying mother's son.

We read of Sarah and her faith,
  Yet childless she in older age
When God provided her a son,
  Her name's inscribed on history's
    page.
We know her life, remember well
  Though Sarah laughed when first
    she heard,
Yet in her faith the promise came
  And now it's written in God's Word.

We read of Mary's humble life;
  How she was blessed with special
    joy;
Respected now in all the world
  For she was mother of God's boy.
And later when He bore the Cross,
  His every thought went out to
    others.
'Twas even then He spoke the word
  That showed His love for faithful
    mothers.

—*E. L. Russell*

5

A Tribute to Mother

Each day I live I want to try
  To be like Mother dear.
I want to have her loving ways,
  Her sunny smile of cheer.

I'd like to learn her patience true,
  For some day when I've grown,
Perhaps I'll have a little home
  And children of my own.

Now when I do, I hope and pray
  That I will prove to be
As kind and good in every way
  As Mother's been to me.

—*Carolyn R. Freeman*

My Mother

Who smoothed my brow;
  Chased away my fears?
Who stood beside me
  All of those years?
    My mother!

Who holds me close;
  Wipes away my tears?
Whenever I call
  Who always hears?
    My mother!

Who loves me still
  When the whole world jeers?
Who helps me stand
  Against my peers?
    My mother!

Who is a gift
  From God above?
Who is a treasure,
  Example of love?
    My mother!

—*Gean D. Smith*

And Time Moves On

Your kids are small, you watch them
  grow,
And all the time you love them so!
School goes by, you make it through,
You follow track and Boy Scouts, too.
You prepare with them for super tests,
For finals—some are real pests!

Before you know, it's graduation time.
You're so proud, feel so sublime!
What'll be next, you begin to wonder.
Will they make it—or go under?
They know the difference between
  good and bad—
You hope—but suddenly you're sad.

Life offers many ways to choose.
The questions: Will they win or lose?
Will they seek a further education?
Or might they choose some other
  station?
Will they get married? And to whom?
Who'll be their bride or future groom?
You have visions for all three,
But sometimes it's not meant to be!

You find yourself so empty-handed!
Like a fish out of water, completely
  stranded.
There's really nothing now you can
  do.
You feel so helpless and a little blue.
Suddenly you come to your senses—
  Look!
It's obvious, Mom, like an open
  book—
The kids are grown; just let them go.
They are the Lord's, and He loves
  them so!

—*Madeleine L. Crighton*

Banquets, Programs, and Sketches

Mother's Day Ideas

by Martha Bolton

Sample Introduction to Your Mother's Day Festivities:

We'd like to welcome each and every one of you to our annual Mother's Day festivities! Now, I don't know how many of you saw me this morning out in the parking lot, but I was busy conducting a survey. I thought it would be interesting to ask some of the women of the church if, on this Mother's Day, they felt appreciated by their husbands. Well—after the first lady I approached laughed hysterically and said, "Appreciated? Are you kidding? I never heard of the word!" I figured I'd better leave well enough alone. I mean if _____ (pastor's wife's name) doesn't feel appreciated, no sense asking anyone else!

Mother's Day Talent Show:

Have talented children of all ages display their musical, dramatic, or artistic talents and dedicate each one to their mother. You could even have an art show in the rear of the church for viewing.

Free Phone Call:

Find out who has a mother living the farthest away, who cannot be present that day. Award that person a free phone call to Mom on Mother's Day!

Mother's Comments:

Have several of your mothers speak a few moments on "My Most Memorable Mother's Day."

Contest:

Why not run a contest to see which mother and daughter look the most alike. (This can be good for a Father's Day contest, too, using father and son.)

A Mother and Child Celebration

by Martha Bolton

(This program includes a lot of participation by children.)

Begin the program with a fashion show of "MOMMIES THROUGH THE AGES." Have the children model old-fashioned dresses of what mother used to wear.

Several weeks before the program, run a "Mother of the Year" contest. Have the children fill out questionnaires on why they feel their mother should win. Not only will this provide you with a winner, but a lot of material for your program as well. Read some of the questionnaires in a "Love Letters to Mom" segment. You may also wish to print up little folders with these letters included. Even mothers who don't win "Mother of the Year" love to know that their child loved them enough to vote for them.

Another cute part of the program is to have children dress up into the "Occupations of a Mother," and repeat the following recitals:

1. *(teacher)* My mother is a
   teacher,
   No summer off has she!
   She's my own live-in tutor
   And she does it all for free!

2. *(chauffeur)* My mom is my
   chauffeur!
   She takes me everywhere I
   go!
   Even when she'd rather be
   Asleep in bed, I know!

3. *(wash woman)* My mommy
   does the ironing
   The washing and the floors!
   The cleaning and the dishes
   Are just more of her FUN
   chores!

4. *(cop)* My mommy's a cop—
   When I fight, she says . . .
   STOP!
   *(Have child hold up a stop
   sign.)*

5. *(seamstress)* My mother is a
   seamstress
   Sewing buttons and bows.
   And she doesn't even get
   thanks
   For all that she sews!

6. *(preacher)* My mother is a
   preacher,
   But Pastor _____ she's
   not!
   (Fill in pastor's name.)
   He only gets ONE HOUR to
   preach,
   All day and night she's got!

7. *(gardener)* My mommy is a
   gardener
   Although her thumb is
   brown,
   She's got the most ambition
   Of anyone in town!

8. *(nurse)* My mommy is a nurse
   She fixes all my little hurts!

8

9. *(cook)* My mommy's a cook
   And a baker and chef.
   I always clean the plate—
   (whispers) It's just the
   vegetables that are left!

10. *(clown)* My mom is a clown,
    She makes me laugh when
    I'm down!

UNISON: "HAPPY MOTHER'S DAY,
           MOM!" *(exit)*

LEADER: And that's only 10 of the different personalities a mother can possess. But it should give us an idea of how much definition is hid in the word *mother!* Webster really took the easy way out when he defined "mother" as a "female parent"! But then, of course, *he* was a man. He wrote a page-and-a-half definition of "father"!

A Special Day in May

by Martha Bolton

Begin your program with the history of Mother's Day:

Mother's Day began when a woman by the name of Anna Jarvis refused to forget her mother. Her mother had passed away, but every year she gathered family and friends together to remember Mama. In 1907, she held a public meeting in Philadelphia, and urged everyone to wear a carnation to remember their mothers. The very first Mother's Day was set on the second Sunday of May, which was May 10 in the year 1908. This was celebrated in Philadelphia only, but in 1914, the president of the United States made it official by setting aside the second Sunday of May each and every year to be Mother's Day. The first national Mother's Day holiday was May 12, 1914.

For your congregational singing, you may wish to take requests from the audience, but say that MOTHERS ONLY can request the songs.

Have the men in your choir or several men in the audience come down the aisles, select a grandmother, have her stand and sing to her. You may wish to have your choir director remain at the microphone to lead the singing. This is a very touching moment, and believe me, there won't be a dry eye in the audience. Especially the grandmothers! Song selections may be made by the choir director or the person in charge of the festivities.

Arrange for three generations of women to give their testimonies. (Grandmother, mother, and daughter.)

Mother's Day is a most appropriate time for baby dedication. Therefore, if there is a couple desiring this, be assured that it fits in beautifully with a Mother's Day program.

I Can Be That Mother
by Esther M. Bailey

Participants needed:

LEADER

FIRST SPEAKER: *describes diligence*

SECOND SPEAKER: *describes strength*

THIRD SPEAKER: *describes honor*

FOURTH SPEAKER: *describes wisdom*

FIFTH SPEAKER: *describes kindness*

SIXTH SPEAKER: *describes reverence*

LEADER: The man of wisdom asked a question, "Who can find a virtuous woman? *(Pause for emphasis)* for her price is far above rubies" *(Proverbs 31:10)*. Then Solomon continued, portraying typical scenes in the life of a good woman. In keeping with the woman's role of that day, the setting was in the home with a supporting cast of children, a husband as costar (or maybe director). It was an upbeat drama incorporating qualities such as diligence, strength, honor, wisdom, kindness, reverence. A note of victory resounded in the conclusion: "Favour is deceitful, and beauty is vain; but a woman that feareth the Lord, she shall be praised" *(Proverbs 31:30)*.

Isn't it wonderful? The value of a virtuous woman is far above rubies! But even more wonderful: *I* can be that woman; *you* can be that woman. External circumstances need not render the power of God ineffective. Christ's promise to provide abundant life extends to today.

If the complexity of the current life-style obstructs the path toward Christian perfection, it also provides greater opportunity for exercise of faith. As the role of women expands, so does opportunity for Christian discipleship. The open field for today's woman allows individual choice.

With freedom of choice, though, comes responsibility. The choice should be made wisely after guideline questions have been answered. Am I choosing a way of life that permits the effecting of my obligations? How can I reconcile what I *want* to do with what I *must* do? In what role can I best carry out my Christian commitment?

Big moments of decision come frequently. Career opportunities, especially the ones requiring extensive preparation, are offered on a rather limited basis. The marriage choice is properly made with a lifetime in mind. The choice of having children is also of major proportions. The chance to make minor decisions, however, happens all the time. It is these matters of lesser impact—everyday ways of moving toward the abundant life—that we want to feature in this program. To prepare our souls for personal receptivity of whatever God has for us during this hour, let us pause for a moment of private reflection and prayer. With bowed heads, may each of us search the hidden recesses of our own heart. *(Pause so that all may silently pray.)* Think about the deepest concern that touches your individual life. Turn the problem over to God . . . allow the mind to anticipate a forthcoming answer that will translate into victorious living in days to come. *(Pause.)* Now, as our own hearts are permeated with the light of Christ, may we turn our thoughts to others . . . family members, coworkers, the stranger who crosses our path. May we now determine that the flame that presently warms our hearts will blaze until it radiates new life to someone we care about. (LEADER *leads in prayer.)*

To further our insight, six of our ladies will comment on the qualities of a virtuous woman as described by Solomon. (LEADER *may now announce the names of all women in consecutive order as they will speak, or a separate introduction may precede each speaker.)*

FIRST SPEAKER: Diligence. Solomon began his treatise by portraying a woman at work: in the domestic realm providing food and clothing for the family, at the marketplace selecting the best buy, even to the buying or selling of property. The efforts of the woman made a difference in how the family lived.

As women reach for and attain new horizons in the work force, there is more opportunity than ever to do something of impacting proportions. Except for restrictions resulting from obligations or a call from God, the field of work is open to choice. And the beneficiary of the effort may be an individual, a corporation, or a large segment of society. Participation in any honorable, worthwhile endeavor is fulfillment of the exhortation to be diligent.

Diligence usually pays off in material blessings, at least to some extent. But honest work coupled with enthusiasm can also enhance the spiritual nature. The exercise of discipline builds character, efforts exerted on behalf of others promote unselfishness, and the joy of ultimate accomplishment provides good reason for thanking the Lord. May we be diligent women. And may we raise our children to be diligent persons.

SECOND SPEAKER: Strength. "She girdeth her loins with strength, and strengtheneth her arms" *(Proverbs 31:17).* Solomon was still talking about a good woman.

Strength can be a physical asset, a natural quality, or the result of training. Physical strength is good, of course, but the strength that characterizes outstanding persons, setting them apart from the ordinary, is the strength that comes from the heart. The apostle Paul spoke of a "strength made perfect in weakness." That kind of strength emanates from an omnipotent God to a person of weakness.

Picture a little boy on an adventure with his father. It's springtime, a beautiful day, and the birds sing sweetly from their perches high in the branches of trees newly revived through God's miracle of the season. The child has strayed a short distance from Daddy, picking wildflowers to take home to Mommy. Suddenly, darkness descends, frightening noises resound in the sky, and streams of water gush to the ground. A moment of panic seizes the child, then he scampers over to jump into Daddy's outstretched arms. Daddy holds his son close to his bosom, covers him with his coat, and carries him to the security of home.

It's that "I-can't-do-it-but-my-Heavenly-Father-can" attitude that marks true strength. If the child had adopted an "I'll-do-it-myself" stance—if he had run in the opposite direction, he would have had to contend alone with elements gone wild. If the child had trusted in personal strength, the job of the father would have been made much more difficult. May we be women who trust in God's strength. And may our children believe in a strength beyond themselves.

THIRD SPEAKER: Honor. Solomon chose the word "honor" as further indication of how a woman of excellence behaves. Good synonyms for honor include honesty, uprightness, truth. Whatever it is called, it's a rare quality in the current scenario. Some people say it's because of turbulent times.

"Inflation corrupts morals," they say, and point to the correlation between an unstable price situation and the tendency to grab what you can before another crisis hits. The link may be there, indeed, but even a situation of dubious outcome isn't reason enough to endorse greed . . . not for the woman of excellence.

Instead of playing the gouging game, the woman of honor will encourage her husband to carefully weigh all factors during a time of wage negotiations. If her employer tries to enlist her cooperation in dishonest or unethical business practices, the woman of honor will stand up for her convictions—change jobs if necessary.

The compromise, if it must come, is better applied to the life-style rather than to the moral code. It's better to cut corners in the standard of living than to jeopardize your claim to a place in the eternal dwelling place of saints. May we be women of honor. May our children be the first to see it in us.

FOURTH SPEAKER: Wisdom. Wisdom is a trait needed to govern the exercise of qualities already presented in this program. If not coupled with wisdom, hard work will result in nothing more than aching muscles. Even the commitment to remain strong for a cause has little value if the cause is chosen unwisely. And how could a woman judge the principles of honesty without an aptitude for discernment?

Some people have greater capacity for sound reasoning than do others. But the talent for judicious appraisal of a matter under consideration can be learned, too. It calls for broad, practical education. Certainly the more facts that are known, the better is the chance for an intelligent evaluation of the situation.

There is a division of thought as to what constitutes wisdom. "For the wisdom of this world is foolishness with God" *(1 Corinthians 3:19a),* wrote Paul. So God doesn't count as wise the individual who neglects personal salvation to achieve material success, no matter how great that success might be. Conversely, the world would consider a woman who sacrifices material benefit for a spiritual cause to be a fool but, actually, she is wise, very wise indeed.

The access route to the heavenly kind of wisdom is through prayer and meditation. Prayer does more than reveal generalities. Through the Holy Spirit's power I can find out what is right for me; you can discover what is right for you. Our part is to fervently seek the Holy Spirit's counsel with complete willingness to act according to the wisdom revealed. May our children be the benefactors of such counsel and guidance.

FIFTH SPEAKER: Kindness. Continuing his theme on a virtuous woman, Solomon wrote, "And in her tongue is the law of kindness" *(Proverbs 31:26b)*. There are many ways to show kindness, all of them important, so it is interesting that Solomon should single out the tongue as the member of the body designated to administer kindness.

Perhaps it was because of the unruly nature of the tongue. It is often easier to give someone a present than it is to speak kind words to that person. "Vain religion" is the way James referred to the faith of a person of unbridled tongue. It's because effects of the Christian testimony can be negated through one careless display of harsh words.

In one respect, at least, the exhortation to kindness is more comprehensive than the love commandment. Sometimes kindness is least extended toward persons most loved, particularly immediate family members. The tendency may be to verify that old familiarity-breeds-contempt axiom. Then it becomes a case of need for retraining. Kindness can become habit just as easily as can the slipshod way of handling close relationships.

A good way to start the retraining program is to bask in the love of God on a personal level. When I recognize God's love emanating toward me, how can I help but pass on some small token of kindness to anyone who shares my domain, especially my children?

SIXTH SPEAKER: Reverence. "A woman that feareth the Lord, she shall be praised" *(Proverbs 31:30b)*. "The fear of the Lord" is a common expression in Solomon's writing as it was in his father David's Book of Psalms. It isn't the debilitating, horrifying kind of fear that's implied. Reverence or wonder is probably better terminology for modern usage.

This deep emotion that a virtuous woman feels from her Creator has no real counterpart in the earthly realm, but a look at an assumed situation will at least start the mind working in the right direction.

Imagine an ordinary woman so favored as to receive invitation for an audience with the queen of England. The experience would probably render the average woman speechless. If this sense of awe could be captured and magnified many times over, it would begin to portray the proper attitude of the human toward the divine.

To continue the analogy, imagine that initial contact developing into a best-friend relationship! Incredible! But so much more amazing is the fact that Jesus Christ died that all human beings could have such a relationship with the Father!

In the Old Testament, a sense of reverence represented the closest possible contact with God for the ordinary person. The apostle Paul spoke of the Spirit of God that dwells within you. It's awe-inspiring to know about God, but it's a foretaste of heaven to *know* God. And that's the one big difference between the religious woman of Solomon's day and the Christian woman of today. We can know God personally. And we can introduce Him to our children.

LEADER: "Who can find a virtuous woman?" Where can she be found? Right here! In our very midst is the potential for contributing more worth to our nation, and to our families, than we can conceive. By tapping the power of God, I can be that woman of value; you can be that woman of immeasurable merit.

(The program may end here with a prayer or dismissal. Or, if the group would like to respond, a time of open expression might be in order.)

The Beginning of Letting Go
A Monologue for Mother's Day

by Gail Blanton

(A woman, preferably dressed in biblical attire, goes to the pulpit or podium.)

This is the beginning. I feel it. I know it. So soon, O God, so soon? I had almost talked myself into believing it was not true. Surely my son was not the Son of God. It must have been some foolish girlhood dream, some quirk of nature. After all, the shepherds, the star, the angels, were so long ago they seemed mere imaginings of an excited, exhausted new mother. Since our trip to Egypt there have been no angels, no visions, no unusual instructions. We live much like any normal family. Surely the Almighty would have special plans for His life, and some proof that we had not misunderstood. But there has only been silence, deep and heavy at first, as I begged for reassurance. Then the silence seemed to weigh on me less and less, and I allowed myself to hope that the old man in the Temple had been wrong. But from time to time the tiniest tip of that sword would softly sting my soul into remembrance. I felt it on that day when Joseph proudly laughed that Jesus would go with him to the carpenter shop and begin to learn a trade. I told Joseph to stop his nonsense, that the boy was much too young. Joseph chuckled as he disagreed, and I instinctively laid a protective hand on Jesus' shoulder. When I saw he meant business I drew my son close to me. Joseph's smile disappeard as he said, "Let the boy go." "No!"—it was almost a cry. Joseph looked sadly surprised, but he gently yet firmly removed my hands as he said, "Mary, let Him go." I watched them go, sobbing. "How silly of me," I thought. But if it was silly, why was I so sad?

And now Joseph says this year we will go to Jerusalem to the Temple. Jesus will become a son of the commandment. A time every family looks forward to, a time we have talked excitedly about and prayed for. Yet, I do not want to go. Again, silly—sad. Again, the sting.

14

You must remember—it has always been my role to be strong enough to protect my son . . . from the beginning, when I first stood to face my parents, then even Joseph. Before He was born, I was determined to protect my son; protect Him from those who did not believe and from those who did believe and would have taken Him to live in a palace. Later that weary trip to Egypt, all to protect my son . . . Surely you see that even though the vision may have faded, I am accustomed to my role. It is instinctive and not easily changed. Joseph seemed to understand my feelings. But he said, "Mary, you are overwrought. It is only a trip to the Temple, and you must let Him go." Yes. It is only that I realize that once I let Him go, He will go and go and go.

> I feel it strike, however slow—
> The beginning of the letting go,
> The bittersweet, the salty flow;
> The parting comes, and must, I know
> That You may give Him back, so
> Dear Father! Help me let Him go.

(Looking more directly at the audience) If you have a son, or a daughter, you know how I feel, or soon will. We must give them up. But don't fear. You see, we give them to One who loves them even more than we do. We give them to God. We give them to God . . .

(It might be appropriate to have the leader close in prayer following the monologue.)

Recitations & Readings

"What Is a Father?"

A father is a good one to brag,
And is always around when time to
play tag,
He helps and teaches each of his
little ones,
And trains them to become a fine
daughter or son.

—*Wanda E. Brunstetter*

Dad Is Special

My dad is special.
Surely you've guessed
Of all the dads
I think he is best.

No other dad
Is like him, you see.
I like to be with him.
He's good company.

—*Merle Glasgow*

Daddy's Little Flower

(for a very tiny little girl)

I'm my daddy's little flower,
I guess I surely must be
For he always says, "You're as sweet as
a rose,"
When he takes me on his knee.

—*Helen Kitchell Evans*

Proud of Me

I know my daddy is proud of me,
He's glad I'm a fine big boy;
I hope I can always please him
And bring him lots of joy.

—*Helen Kitchell Evans*

My Wonderful Dad

My dad explains
Many things to me
That I don't understand
But he does, you see.

I ask him questions,
I guess, by the score;
He is always so patient
And ready for more.

He's a wonderful dad,
That's plain to see;
I'm glad God chose him
As the dad for me.

—*Merle Glasgow*

Our Heroes

Some kids admire Abe Lincoln
And some George Washington;
Some admire Napoleon
For the battles he has won;
But me, I admire my dad
And I am proud to be his son.

—*Rega Kramer McCarty*

16

What Is a Father?

A father is someone who loves me
　Who gives me a hug every day;
A father is someone who cares
　Where I go, what I do, where I play.

A father is someone who works
　For all of our family;
A father is someone I know
　Loves my mother, my sister, and me.

　　　　　　　—Helen Kitchell Evans

My Father

My father is a busy man
　But he has time each day
To listen when I talk to him—
　That is just his way.

And if I ask him questions
　I know for sure that he
Will take the time to answer them—
　He knows so much, you see.

God bless my father every day;
　He means so much to me;
I hope when I grow up
　His kind of man I'll be.

　　　　　　　—Merle Glasgow

Like My Dad

You set good examples for me,
　You are my guiding light;
You're always there to help me
　And keep me going right.

You believe in peace
　And brotherhood for all;
You believe in Jesus
　And will answer to His call.

I hope I can repay you
　For the many things you do;
I know I'll grow up happy
　If I can be like you.

　　　　　　　—Helen Kitchell Evans

My Dad

I think my dad's the very best
　Of all the dads I know.
He taught me how to catch a ball
　And also how to throw.
I like to help him wash the car
　And make it shine so bright;
I like it when he hears my prayers
　And tucks me in at night.
When I grow up I want to be
　A man just like my dad
Because I think my dad's the best
　A fellow ever had.

　　　　　　　—Lucy Hamilton

Extra Cheer

We're very glad to see you
　In our church today;
We welcome all the family,
　But I just want to say
There is a special welcome
　For all the fathers here.
There are so many out today
　Let's give them an extra cheer!

(Child claps hands so that the congre-
gation does likewise.)

　　　　　　　—Helen Kitchell Evans

Best of All

There's a day set aside for children,
　A day for mothers, too;
A day set aside for promotion,
　A day for Thanksgiving, too.

But the best day of all I think
　Is when I can stand here and say,
"I have a wonderful father
　To greet on Father's Day."

　　　　　　　—Helen Kitchell Evans

Want a Pal?

Want a day of fishing?
  Well, get a pal like Dad!
Want a day of hiking?
  He's the best friend you've ever had.
Want to see the sights?
  Call on Dad to go with you;
He can be the best of pals
  In everything you do!

—Rega Kramer McCarty

I Want to Be like Dad

I really want to be like Dad.
  I think he's quite a man;
He goes to Sunday School and church
  As often as he can.

He's honest as the day is long.
  He always tells the truth.
I know I want to be like him,
  A pattern for all youth.

The reason why I follow him:
  He's following our Lord;
And so he'll never lead astray
  From God's most Holy Word.

—E. L. Russell

What Is a Father?

1ST CHILD: What is a father? Who is he?
2ND CHILD: He provides for us, his family.
3RD CHILD: He works so hard for us all each day,
4TH CHILD: And he cares for us much in every way.

1ST CHILD: *My* father helps me fly a kite!
2ND CHILD: *Mine* helps me throw a ball just right!
3RD CHILD: *My* father mends my broken toys!
4TH CHILD: *Mine* shares my sorrow and my joys!

1ST CHILD: *My* father helps me ride my bike.
2ND CHILD: *Mine* takes me on a woodland hike!
3RD CHILD: *Mine* teaches me God's loving ways
4TH CHILD: And *mine* shows me how to give Him praise!

UNISON: We're here to say we're very glad
For everybody's special dad!
And that is why we proudly say,
Happy, happy Father's Day!

*—Jean Conder Soule and
Mildred Johnson*

Father

A father doesn't push, he leads.
A father doesn't dictate, he guides.
A father doesn't need to preach—
  His life is his sermon.
A father doesn't criticize the bad in his children;
  He encourages the good.
A father doesn't seek respect, he earns it.
A father doesn't ask for love—
  He's rewarded it.
A father doesn't bargain his children's welfare,
  He provides it.
A father doesn't worry about tomorrow—
  He trusts God for it.

—Martha Bolton

A Psalm for Fathers

Blessed is the man that becometh a
    father
And delighteth in his offspring;
Who looketh upon his newborn with
    pride,
    And feeleth the joy that such a
    moment can bring!

Blessed is that father who taketh the
    hand of his toddler
    And tenderly helpeth him to walk
    upright;
Who shareth with the mother the
    anguish of illness,
    And the sleeplessness of a troubled
    night.

Blessed is the father who sendeth his
    child to school
    And cooperateth with the teacher.
Who taketh his children, be they
    many or few,
    Each week to listen to a good
    preacher.

Blessed is that father who
    instructeth his children
    To work when they are yet small;
Who causeth them to feel it is
    honorable to labor
    When they have grown tall!

Blessed is that father who teacheth
    his children
    Patience and understanding to all
    men.
Who helpeth them to love the sinner,
    But to hate the sin!

Blessed is that father who instilleth
    in his children
    The desire to learn to their fullest
    capacity;
Who striveth to develop in them
    through life
    Traits of goodness and veracity.

Blessed is the father who prepareth
    his children for marriage,
    And letteth them go to live their
    own lives;
Who, by his example, hath made
    them determined
    To choose good husbands or wives!

Blessed is that man who becometh a
    grandfather
And knoweth all of the joys
Of being what that name implies
    To his children's girls and boys.

Blessed, yea, blessed is that man!

            —*Blanche Bliss Butler*

'Specially Mine!

You've heard our program
    We're almost through,
And we have liked it,
    Didn't you?
We sang our sweetest
    Songs of praise
And said we love you
    Lots of ways.
No fathers could be
    Half as fine
As you dear fathers—
    'Specially mine!

—*Dorothy Conant Stroud*

We Want You to Know

I'm a little bit timid,
    But so very proud
To stand at attention
    Before this big crowd.
We want you to know, dads,
    That we think you're nice;
We wouldn't exchange you
    For millions in price!

—*Dorothy Conant Stroud*

My Dad

(For a boy)

I thank You, Father, for my dad,
I want to make him see
How very much I value him
And what he does for me.

I thank You for his honesty,
His kindness, and his care;
I thank You for his trust in me,
And secrets that we share.

And when I make mistakes,
My dad will hold my hand;
I have his love and confidence,
For he can understand.

My daddy is my partner,
On whom I can depend;
I honor him and love him,
And he's my special friend!

Lord, help me grow up manly,
And may I sometime be
The hero of some other boy
That my dad is to me!

—*Nona Keen Duffy*

Mended

See my pretty doll,
She's just as good as new;
Once she was my mother's,
She played with her, too.

She looked pretty bad
When we took her from the shelf,
But my daddy went to work,
Now she looks like herself.

My daddy's pretty wonderful;
He's clever as can be.
He mended arms and legs;
Now she belongs to me.

Aren't fathers marvelous?
I just want to say,
"I sure love you, Daddy
On this Father's Day."

—*Helen Kitchell Evans*

The Lessons from a Shoe

1ST BOY *(pointing to the tongue of a shoe):*
The human tongue is not so large,
But it is often heard;
So we must very careful be
In choosing every word.

2ND BOY *(pointing to heel):*
I would not call a man a heel.
That has an awful sound;
But I must keep my feet secure
While walking on the ground.

3RD BOY *(pointing to toe of shoe):*
To toe the mark is really good,
To walk the narrow road;
So I shall toe the Scripture mark
And walk as Jesus showed.

4TH BOY *(pointing to sole of shoe):*
This shoe has never lost its sole,
But what a mighty cost
When men are careless with their souls
And find them truly lost.

5TH BOY *(pointing to the whole shoe and turning it around):*
The tongue, the sole, the heel, the toe.
Be careful, I repeat;
For we must live as Jesus lived
With dedicated feet.

—*E. L. Russell*

Almost as Wonderful

With tributes to our loving dads
The whole day we could fill,
And though my dad is wonderful
And kind and good, I will
Take most of my time to say
There is another who
Is almost just as wonderful—
It's Grandpa! Guess you knew!

—*Dorothy Conant Stroud*

Sketches

A Baseball Glove

by James Mulholland

Cast:
FATHER: *A loving father who has underestimated the faith of his son.*
ANDY: *An unusual little boy with a big heart.*

Costume Note:
Casual dress. Baseball cap for ANDY.

Props:
Small paper sack
A baseball glove

Production Notes:
ANDY can be portrayed by an adult or teenager. Children love to see others act like children.

(The front porch of a house. On the steps sits ANDY, *eight years old, looking into a paper sack. His* FATHER *enters with a baseball glove in his hand.)*

FATHER: Want to play catch, Andy?

ANDY *(quickly hiding the sack):* Naw.

FATHER *(surprised):* No. What's wrong? Are you sick?

ANDY: No. I just don't feel like it.

FATHER *(sitting down next to* ANDY): Well, what do you feel like?

ANDY: I don't know.

(They sit in silence for a moment.)

ANDY *(nervously):* Dad, would you be really mad at me if I lost my baseball glove?

FATHER *(angrily):* What? You mean you lost your glove?

ANDY *(quickly):* No.

FATHER (*suspiciously*): Then why did you ask me if I'd be mad?

ANDY: I just wondered.

FATHER: Andy, where is your baseball glove?

ANDY (*sighing*): I don't have it no more.

FATHER (*upset*): Come on, Andy. Stop playing games. Just admit it. You were careless and you lost your glove.

ANDY (*defensively*): I wasn't careless. I gave it to somebody.

FATHER (*disgusted*): What? You mean you loaned somebody that brand-new glove that cost us almost $20.00?

ANDY: I didn't loan it.

FATHER (*confused*): Well, what did you do then?

ANDY (*reluctantly*): Well, I sort of gave it away.

FATHER (*losing control*): Gave it away! To who?

ANDY: Billy Johnson.

FATHER (*sternly*): Well, young man, tomorrow morning you're going to march right up to Billy Johnson and demand your glove back.

(ANDY *bows his head in obvious misery.*)

ANDY: Do I have to?

FATHER: Of course. You don't give your things away.

ANDY: Why not?

FATHER: Well, because . . . well, because you don't. I mean, Andy, why did you give it away? Did you trade it for something?

ANDY: Well, yeah.

FATHER (*disgusted*): I thought so. What?

(ANDY *pulls out the paper sack and hesitantly hands it to his* FATHER. *His* FATHER *opens it to look inside.*)

FATHER (*shocked*): Three marbles, some bottle caps, and a baseball card? This is what you traded for that glove?

ANDY (*defensively*): That's all he had to trade.

FATHER: And you just had to trade?

ANDY: No, but he liked my glove so much and he didn't have one.

FATHER: Do you always give your things away to people who like them?

ANDY: No, just to Billy.

FATHER: What's so special about Billy?

ANDY: He's my best friend.

FATHER: Well, you tell your best friend to have his dad buy him his own glove.

ANDY: Billy doesn't have a dad, and his mom never has any money. He doesn't have any friends 'cause he wears real old clothes and they're always dirty. I'm Billy's friend and . . .

FATHER *(still angry):* So you felt sorry for him and gave him your glove.

ANDY: Yeah, 'cause in Sunday School they told us that Jesus said that if somebody asks you for your coat, you're supposed to give it to them.

FATHER *(trapped):* Well, did Billy ask for your glove?

ANDY: No.

FATHER *(uncomfortable):* Well, then you shouldn't have given it to him.

ANDY *(about to cry):* I guess I just wanted Billy to be happy. I told him how happy I was 'cause you bought me my glove and he said he wished he had a dad to give him things. So I just thought having my glove might make him happy. I'm sorry, Dad. I'll make him give it back tomorrow.

(ANDY *bows his head while his* FATHER *squirms uncomfortably with the sudden realization that his son doesn't deserve his anger.)*

FATHER *(putting his arm around* ANDY): No, Andy. You're right . . . I was wrong.

(ANDY *looks up in surprise.)*

FATHER: Jesus does want us to give to others. Even baseball gloves. I'm very proud of you. I'm glad I have a son who cares enough about his friend to give him his baseball glove.

ANDY *(hopefully):* Then Billy can keep my glove?

FATHER *(laughing):* Yes. I'll tell you what. Why don't you see if Billy can come over tomorrow and play catch with us?

ANDY *(excited):* Really, Dad? That would be great.

FATHER: Of course, we'll just have two gloves.

ANDY: Well, you can hit 'em to us.

FATHER *(smiling):* All right.

ANDY *(sighing happily):* Boy, I can't wait to tell Billy that I get to share my dad with him.

(FATHER *and* ANDY *both smile.)*

I'm So Inadequate, Lord

by V. Louise Cunningham

Cast:

BARRY PETERS: *A young man who feels inadequate and doubts that his life counts for very much. Leader of teenage boys and father of two young sons.*

JORDAN: *Has a father who abuses him.*

TERRY: *Terry's parents are thinking about divorce.*

SHAWN: *A class member.*

DOUG: *His father doesn't see anything wrong with cheating on income tax or speeding. He's in class but doesn't really participate.*

GRANT: *A teenage boy converted at camp.*

TYLER: *A bully.*

MITCHELL: *A bully.*

JOHN: *A fellow teacher.*

Setting:
The stage is divided. The larger left side is Barry Peters' Sunday School room and the right side is used for action by the boys in his class.

Scene I

(Classroom scene. BARRY is in front of the class of boys. GRANT, TYLER, and MITCHELL are still offstage. The rest of the boys are talking among themselves and doing a little pushing and shoving to find their seats. JORDAN and TERRY sit together, JORDAN on outside of row. When BARRY begins to pray, the boys stop in mid-action.)

BARRY: Dear Father, please send someone else to work with these boys. It's not that I don't care, but these young men face such a different world than I did, and I'm so inadequate. *(Turns to face class and the boys, action resumes.)* We're running a little late, so if you will find a place to sit, we can begin. Boys . . . All right, Jordan, sit down please. *(He reaches out to touch JORDAN's shoulder.)*

(JORDAN draws back like BARRY was going to hit him.)

24

BARRY *(takes back his hand. Freeze action):* O Lord, how could I have forgotten. Jordan thought I was going to beat him like his father does. I remember last week when we were talking about God being a loving Father, Jordan couldn't understand. He has never known what it means to be loved and cared for properly. How can people do that to their children? *(Pause.)* Lord, help me to keep control of myself and not ever lash out at anyone in anger. Help me to administer discipline with love to my two sons. I don't ever want to see the pain in my boys' eyes that I see in Jordan's.

(Action resumes. Class settles down.)

BARRY: Will you read our Scripture lesson for today, Terry. Matthew 22:36-40.

TERRY *(opens Bible and finds his place. Starts reading strongly; but when it comes to section on love, his voice falters):* "Teacher, which is the greatest commandment in the Law? Jesus replied: 'Love the Lord your God with all your heart, with all your soul and with all your mind.' This is the first and greatest commandment. And the second is like it: 'Love your neighbor as yourself.' All the Law and the Prophets hang on these two commandments" (NIV).

(Freeze action.)

BARRY: Lord, I've done it again. How could I have asked Terry to read anything dealing with love when he is so upset over his parents getting a divorce. I know his grades have fallen and his attitude in class has changed with all the upheaval going on in his life. Lord, what am I going to do now? I don't want to make Terry feel any worse, but I want these young men to understand about loving neighbors and their wives when they get married. Dear Father, I pray for openness in my marriage. I know I tend to keep things to myself and that shuts off communication with my wife. Help us to keep those lines open between us. How can I help these boys who are so hurt by their parents?

(Action resumes.)

TERRY: Mr. Peters, Jesus said we were to love our neighbor as ourselves. How come my folks who used to love each other quit? Everybody thinks they are such good Christians. Why aren't they trying to love each other?

BARRY: Terry has a real good question. What does the Bible say about love? Is love a feeling or an act of the will? *(Walks around classroom and ends up by* JORDAN.)

JORDAN *(he nudges* TERRY, *whispers):* You OK?

TERRY *(whispers):* Yeah.

BARRY *(he notices* JORDAN's *nudge and asks question of* JORDAN *to get his attention without thinking):* Do you have an answer for us Jordan on love?

JORDAN: Who, me, no. I don't know much about love.

TERRY: What does all this mean about love anyhow? Jesus talked about loving neighbors, but what about husbands and wives? I thought when people got married they stayed married. All my folks do is fight, and now they're talking divorce. What happened to love? I don't understand.

BARRY: Parents aren't perfect . . .

TERRY *(interrupts):* Have you ever thought about divorce?

BARRY *(slowly answers to have time to think):* No. I haven't been married that long, but I would like to think I would resist temptation and flee to God's arms when the time came. There is so much pressure from the secular world now as far as our moral values. Remember my question, is love a feeling or an act of the will?

SHAWN *(volunteers):* It's an act of the will. We can decide we will love.

BARRY: That's right, and then our emotions and feelings will come later.

JORDAN: My dad's feelings of love come after he has knocked me against the wall a few times. I don't understand when you talk about God being a loving Father. Man, I don't need another loving father. The one I have is enough.

BARRY: I know it's hard to understand. God *is* a loving Father. We are to try to be like Him.

JORDAN: Do you ever get really mad at your kids and spank them hard and stuff?

BARRY: I guess sometimes my children think I do. Many times they don't realize what I am trying to teach them when I have to discipline them.

GRANT *(comes in excited, hair is mussed and shirt out of pants):* God is so good.

SHAWN: What are you so excited about?

GRANT: I was on my way here today and you know Tyler and Mitchell. They were going to give me a bad time about coming here. Tyler grabbed my Bible from me.

SHAWN: Welcome to the real world of being a Christian.

GRANT: But wait till I tell you what happened. It was a real answer to prayer.

(Freeze action. GRANT *moves on the other side of the stage where* TYLER *and* MITCHELL *are waiting.* TYLER *and* MITCHELL *are pushing* GRANT *around.* GRANT *is carrying his Bible.)*

TYLER: Look at the Jesus freak, Mitchell.

MITCHELL: He doesn't go anywhere without his Bible anymore.

TYLER: He's no fun anymore. He doesn't want to be part of our gang now.

(MITCHELL *grabs Bible away from* GRANT.)

GRANT: Come on guys, give me back my Bible. I don't want to be late.

TYLER: You going to church, preacher man. *(Taunts.)* Let's hear your sermon.

MITCHELL *(says to* TYLER): Here, catch.

GRANT: No, don't do that to my Bible. *(Tries to get it away from* MITCHELL.)

(MITCHELL *passes the Bible to* TYLER. *They continue to pass it back and forth while* GRANT *tries to get it.* GRANT *quits trying and stands still.)*

TYLER *(jabs at* GRANT *with the Bible):* What are you doing, praying, Jesus freak? Here's your Holy Book, preacher man.

MITCHELL: Aw, come on. He's no fun anymore anyhow. Let's go.

(TYLER *lays the Bible down at* GRANT's *feet.)*

GRANT: Why don't you come to church with me and see what a difference Christ can make in your life.

MITCHELL *and* TYLER: You've got to be kidding. *(Laugh and exit.)*

GRANT *(leans over and picks up his Bible):* Mr. Peters said there would be hard times, but I didn't know it would be like this, Lord. *(Tucks his Bible under his arm and heads for class.)*

(Freeze action.)

BARRY: Lord, it was a real answer to prayer for Grant to accept You as his Savior at camp. It isn't going to be easy for Grant now. He was so upset when his alcoholic parents laughed at him. How can he grow strong in his Christian life and learn to be a man after Your own heart against all these obstacles? I pray for his strength.

(Action resumes.)

GRANT: I can see this Christian life isn't going to be easy. But Jesus said we are to love our enemies. You know, Mitchell was right. When I quit trying to get my Bible away from them and started praying for them, they gave me my Bible and left.

SHAWN: Don't think it is always going to be that easy.

(Freeze action.)

BARRY: Lord, how can I help Doug understand that loving a neighbor as ourselves relates to honesty in all areas of our life? His father, Fred, is such a poor example for him. All he does is brag about how he cheats on his income tax and his unfair business practices.

(Action resumes; bell rings.)

BARRY: Well, that's all the time we have today. Those of you who haven't memorized Matthew 22:37-40 for next week ... *(Calls after them as boys exit.)* Bye. *(Stretches out hand as if to reach them in some way.)*

(Boys all holler "bye" and shuffle out.)

BARRY: Lord, what did anybody learn today in the short time we had. We didn't cover the lesson, and I know that Jordan and Terry must be really upset with me. *(Buries his head in his hands.)*

(Freeze action.)

(SHAWN and DOUG go to right side of stage and sit on chairs, pretending to be in a car. DOUG is in driver's seat.)

SHAWN: Aren't you going a little fast? Speed limit here is only 45.

DOUG *(looks at speedometer):* So I'm doing 55, that's the way my dad drives along here. Besides, the cops don't radar this area anymore.

SHAWN: That's not the point.

DOUG: You're going to tell me God cares, right?

SHAWN: Right. We are told we are to obey the laws of the land unless it is contrary to God's commands.

DOUG: But my dad says it is dumb for this stretch of road to be posted at 45.

SHAWN: That doesn't make any difference. God wants us to obey. If we don't like the laws, then we should try to change them, not disobey them.

DOUG: You sound just like Mr. Peters.

SHAWN: Are you going to slow down?

DOUG: I will for you.

SHAWN: I don't want you to do it for me but for God.

DOUG: OK, so I'll slow down. I'll even think about what you said. Now let's talk about our basketball team. Do you think we have a chance this year to go to State?

(Action resumes.)

JOHN *(enters):* I thought you might be gone, Barry.

BARRY: Yes, John. I'm praying for my boys. Do you ever feel totally inadequate to minister to your group of boys?

JOHN: All the time, Barry, all the time.

BARRY: What do you do?

JOHN: I do the best I know how and then do what you're doing. I pray. My guess is that we won't know this side of heaven how the Lord has used us.

BARRY *(slowly, thoughtfully):* Maybe you're right, maybe you're right. It sure would be good to know if I have been able to help anyone.

JOHN: I'm going home now. When you leave, will you lock the door? Bye, Barry.

BARRY: Bye, John. *(Goes back to his praying.)* Lord, use me in the lives of these young men You have brought into my life. Help me to minister to them for You. I'll try to do the best I can with Your help.

(Light fades as BARRY continues praying.)

The Best Present

by V. Louise Cunningham

Cast:
BRAD: *A rather quiet, thoughtful child*
EMILY: *Feelings are easily hurt*
JUSTIN: *Very interested in mechanical things*
SARA: *Spoiled, thinks she is really something*
MATT: *Father of* BRAD
JOHN: *Father of* EMILY
RICH: *Father of* JUSTIN
DWIGHT: *Father of* SARA, *thinks he is something special*

Scene I

(The four children are talking among themselves. They are sitting at a table and have paper and pencils or crayons.)

BRAD: What are you going to give your dads for Father's Day? It's going to be here pretty soon.

EMILY: I'm going to paint a design on a T-shirt. I haven't decided what I'll put on it yet. Maybe a horse.

JUSTIN: Dads don't want a dumb horse on a T-shirt.

SARA: That's not a dumb idea. Emily can draw horses real good.

JUSTIN: Men would rather have cars or trucks on T-shirts.

EMILY: Maybe I could just write something on it like Happy Father's Day or World's Best Dad.

SARA *(bragging):* I'm going to give my dad the grass catcher for our new lawn mower.

JUSTIN: You don't get that big an allowance.

SARA: That doesn't matter. I'm going to sign my name to a card and put it on the grass catcher. What are you going to give your dad, Brad?

BRAD: I don't know. I'm trying to get some ideas because I don't have any money.

EMILY: Not even for a T-shirt? They don't cost very much.

BRAD: I know, but ever since Mom was in the hospital we don't have any extra money.

SARA: What are you going to give your father, Justin?

JUSTIN: I haven't thought about it. We're going to make tie-dye hankies at school and maybe Mom would help me make his favorite kind of cookies.

EMILY *(has been drawing a picture and holds it up):* How do you like this for a T-shirt design?

JUSTIN: I've never seen a car like that before.

EMILY: Of course not, it's a fantasy car.

SARA: Looks like a nightmare to me.

EMILY: Well, let's see you draw something better. *(Almost in tears.)*

BRAD: It's not that bad. Can I show you what would help a little?

EMILY: Sure. *(Hands him the paper.)*

BRAD *(works on paper):* If you shorten this line a little and make this a little longer, I think that will help.

EMILY: That does look better. Thanks, Brad.

BRAD: If you want you could add a little something more to the grill, you could make it a face or . . .

EMILY: You mean like this? *(Draws a few lines on the paper.)*

JUSTIN: That's good! I wonder if I could put a car or something on the hankie rather than just writing Happy Father's Day or something dumb on it.

SARA: Well, my dad is going to thank me everytime he uses the lawn mower.

JUSTIN: During the winter he won't think about your present because he won't have to cut the grass. My dad will think of me everytime he uses his hankie.

SARA: Yeah, to blow his nose on it. *(Laughs unkindly.)*

Scene II

(The four men are at an office.)

RICH: I don't see any bright new Father's Day ties. Don't tell me none of you got one.

MATT: No, not this year.

JOHN: I didn't think it was appropriate to wear my present.

RICH: Why, did you get some new tools instead of something to wear?

JOHN: No, it's a T-shirt with a fantasy car on it. Emily did a real good job of drawing.

DWIGHT: It will probably come off the first time you wash it.

JOHN: No, I don't think so. It's something new to paint on shirts. It has a puffy look to it. What did you get, Rich?

RICH: Cars must be the in thing. Justin put a car on a hankie and then it was dyed.

DWIGHT: I got a new lawn mower and grass catcher. Sara gave me the grass catcher.

RICH: She must have a pretty big allowance. *(Pause.)* A lawn mower sounds like work to me. *(Laughs.)*

DWIGHT: Sara got money from my wife, but I still think I got the best present.

JOHN: We haven't heard what Matt got for Father's Day yet.

MATT: It wasn't anything like a lawn mower, but I think it was the best present a man could receive.

DWIGHT: It will have to go some to beat out my lawn mower.

JOHN: I don't know about that. I got a designer-made shirt.

MATT: I got a very special card.

DWIGHT *(sarcastically):* Boy, that is real nice!

MATT: I just happened to bring it with me. Just look at this. *(Gives it to* DWIGHT *to read.)*

DWIGHT: This is going to be good. *(He starts out jokingly and then gets more serious.)* "Dear Dad, I couldn't think of anything special enough to get you so I'm writing this card. I want to thank you, Dad, for taking me fishing; I like to be alone with you. I liked the time we sat around the campfire and sang silly songs. Thank you, Dad, for coming in with Mom every night to listen to my prayers. It's fun when you stay and read a story to me and then tuck me in. I'm so glad God gave me you for my dad. I hope you have a special day. You're the best Dad anybody could have!!!!!!!

Love, Brad."

RICH: I guess that is the best present.

DWIGHT *(hands back the card):* Beats out a grass catcher any day. *(Thoughtfully, bragging spirit gone.)* You really took time with Brad to build loving memories.

MATT *(takes card and puts in back in his pocket):* It isn't always easy, but I try.

A New Bike

by Helen Kitchell Evans

(As the scene opens, SALLY and JANE are talking.)

SALLY: Are you going to get that bike you wanted?

JANE: No, my father said no.

SALLY: Guess you are pretty disappointed.

JANE: Sure, wouldn't you be?

SALLY: I guess so. Why did he say no?

JANE: He didn't give me a reason. That's the way my dad is.

SALLY: Mine, too. Guess all dads are like that. How long has it been since you asked him?

JANE: Oh, about a week.

SALLY: Here comes your dad now. Look what he is rolling up the sidewalk!

(Enter FATHER with bike.)

FATHER: I saw you looking. How do you like it?

JANE: I don't understand. You said that I couldn't have that bike.

FATHER: Sure I did, but I didn't say that you could not have *a* bike. The one you wanted was too big for you. I just felt that I knew what was best for you at your age.

SALLY: You know, that's a little like praying and not getting the answer you want.

JANE: Maybe that's because God has something better in mind for us.

FATHER: Good thinking, girls. God does know what is best for each of us. He answers prayer but it's . . .

SALLY: Yeah! It's not always the way we want the prayer answered.

FATHER: Come on, let's see Jane ride this new bike. The training wheels are still on it.

JANE: I don't need those things. I'm no baby!

SALLY: Better think, Jane. Maybe your dad knows best. He can take them off in a few days. It might save you from a hard fall until you get the hang of it.

JANE: OK. Let's go! THANKS, DAD!

(All exit.)

God Needs Helpers

KATHRYN BLACKBURN PECK

FAITH CHAMBERS WILSON

1. God needs help - ers, will - ing help - ers,
2. God needs help - ers, man - y help - ers;

Bus - y all the days;
There is much to do,

Help - ing moth - ers, help - ing oth - ers
Mak - ing oth - er peo - ple hap - py.

In all sorts of ways.
I will help. Will you?

Everlasting Love

G. A.

Glen Aubrey

1, 3. When I want to know how God loves —
2. La, la, la, la, la, la, la, la, la,

me, I just look at my mom-my's love — and I see! Kind and ten-der,
la, la, la, la, la, la, la, la, la, la, la, la. La, la, la, la,

full and free; That's the way my mom-my and God love me.
la, la, la. La, la, la, la, la, la, la

la, la, la. God love me! That's the way my mom-my and

God love me. —

My Heavenly Father's Care

RUTH GIBBS ZWALL

EVELYN F. TARNER

1. I am glad God gives to me Home and friends and fam - i - ly. Ev - 'ry gift that's from a - bove Shows my Heav'n - ly Fa - ther's love.
2. Ev - 'ry gift He sends is good, All my cloth - ing, all my food; Ev - 'ry world He made so fair Shows my Heav'n - ly Fa - ther's care.
3. I am glad be - cause I know That He loves His chil - dren so. And this I will thank Him as I pray For the gifts He gives each day.

Christian Families

S. H. C.

SUZANNE H. CLASON

1. Je - sus had a fam - 'ly just like you and me;_____ Some - times His dad,
2. Mar - y cooked His good meals, made Him His new clothes,_____ Taught Him how to
3. Je - sus had fun play - ing when He was a boy,_____ Shar - ing with His
4. Each day they would gath - er, pray and read God's Word._____ Ev - 'ry - thing was

Jo - seph, bounced Je - sus__ on his knee.
live right, just__ as the__ Bi - ble shows.
play - mates ev - 'ry game and__ each new toy.
put up, God's__ Ho - ly__ Word was heard.

Refrain

Christ - ian fam - 'lies serve the__ Lord and live for

Him each day; Lord Je - sus, lead our

own fam - 'ly in Your ho - ly way.